A Sparrow's Perspective

The Poetry of Kathy Earsman

A catalogue record for this book is available from the National Library of Australia

First published in 2021
Copyright © Kathleen Earsman, 2021

Paperback ISBN: 978-0-6452994-0-3
Ebook ISBN: 978-0-6452994-1-0
Published in Australia
All inquiries should be made to the author. Email: kathyearsman@hotmail.com
Cover design: Barry Earsman
Interior design: Adrian Anderson

Dedicated to my husband, Peter William Earsman
and our sons, Barry, Matthew and Travis.

PREFACE

'How would you like about half a dozen unfinished letters?'

I'd discovered I had four days off from my job as a trainee nurse. That was rare enough to take me into Auckland City that night. There, I caught a Greyhound bus to Waiouru, a military camp where my friends Lynne and Larry Southern lived. It was very late and snowing when I arrived, but their door wasn't locked. I went in and curled up on the sofa, giving them quite a shock to see me in the morning.

Larry insisted I meet his friend Peter, so I went along to a celebration at the mess hall. When Peter walked in, I was besotted. It turned out he felt the same way. When I had to return to Auckland, Peter put me on the train, promising he'd write. But he didn't.

Surprisingly, I got another three-day break from duty, so I went back to Waiouru to see what was going on. Larry brought Pete around to the house. We sat on the steps, and he said the one thing that changed everything: 'How would you like about half a dozen unfinished letters?' We exchanged lots of letters after that, and were married five months later, in 1967. Soon after, he went to Vietnam and I finished my nursing training.

The news about Vietnam was terrifying, but he returned safely. We moved to Wellington, where our sons Barry and Matthew were born, then to Waiouru, relocating to Singapore in the early 1970s to follow Peter's Army posting there. Our youngest son Travis was born there, as well as some of my most interesting poems.

By the 1990s we were living in Australia. Peter had won a poetry competition and began writing more often on the computer. He seemed to be always peering at the screen. I missed his company, so I pulled up a chair and joined him. Side by side we sat, my computer slaved to his, and so began our journey into online poetry sites.

We found OzPoet, Haiku Hut, Aha! Poetry, the Sonnet Board, Yellow Moon Publications and many others. We made a lot of friends around the world, some of whom we met in person. We were published on various forums and in books, several of which were sent to us with inscriptions. We even won some prizes. Pete and I were published in 'Poems of Distant

Wars', and the International War Veterans' Poetry Archives, which was especially significant to him, I think.

It was during this time that I developed a love of metered and other poetry. I learned how to compose many forms including sonnets, free verse and Japanese poetry; haiku, haibun, and several other forms. It was an exciting time. Peter and I shared our verses with each other and our online friends around the world.

Years passed. Shockingly, in 2004, my husband died. Dad asked me to go to New Zealand to help him with my sick mother. I stayed with my parents and helped for as long as I could, until my son Matt invited me to join him in Nepal.

Sometime later, I moved to Maleny to be near my family and continued to work as a registered nurse. I subsequently became a wildlife rescuer and carer. Life was hard without Peter, but I tried to stay creative and engaged in my local community.

In early 2021, I met author and editor Leigh Robshaw, who generously facilitated the publication of this book. Our long-time family friend Adrian Anderson worked on the interior design and my three sons, Barry, Matthew and Travis were also key contributors.

A Sparrow's Perspective is a collection of works from my life. It incorporates a lot of different eras, both with Peter and without him. My favourite pieces are the ones I wrote during those golden years, sitting by his side, writing poetry together.

I dearly hope you enjoy them.

Definitions:

Sonnet – A rhymed poem in iambic pentameter. There are many prescribed forms, with differing rhymes and stanza breaks signalling a shift in focus. The form most used in this book (the English or Shakespearean sonnet), has three quatrains and a couplet, presented in a block of fourteen lines.

Introduction: two quatrains (eight lines in which a subject or situation is described), with a volta or 'turn' at line eight.

A third quatrain, where a change occurs within the next four lines that describe a shift in perspective.

Conclusion: a couplet, i.e. two lines that complete the sonnet, often in a surprising way.

Example:

A Spanish Drunk

Before his morning-after starts to pound,
before he's isolated by the crowd
he claims the curb, his body bent around
an agony of song; he cries aloud
in passionate flamenco, ages old.
His voice is patinated cobblestones
and honey-leather saddles glowing gold,
his voice is aching muscles, crumbled bones.
It translates somewhere primal where I hide.　　　　　(volta)
My breath is stopped. His ardour kindles flames
where ice has held me since my own love died
and flays me with the richness that he claims.
Ironically the poet in my head　　　　　(couplet)
will never understand a word he said.

Iambic Pentameter – Iambs form the rhythm of the poem; unstressed/stressed, unstressed/stressed for ten beats, i.e. five groups of stressed/unstressed.

Example: the DAY/has COME/and TIME/has SLIPPED/aWAY/

Pentameter refers to that beat of five metrical feet. Each beat is called a 'foot'.

Haiku – Japanese in origin, it is said to be the most rule-driven poem in the world. Unfortunately, it was wrongly presented by the first English describers of haiku, including the assumption that it is written in 5,7,5 English syllables. But Japanese verse counts sound units known as on or morae. Although there may be 17 of them, they are much shorter. Other Japanese rules were also not mentioned. English haiku has subsequently become diverse in structure.

Traditionally, the poem includes a kigo, which indicates a season. They are drawn from a comprehensive list called a saijiki and are quite specific. A Japanese 'cutting word' is required. It is not actually a word, but often a dash that juxtaposes the first image with the second. Haiku focus on a brief moment, into which the reader enters and experiences a sense of revelation or understanding. Often there is a sense of 'aha!'

The poet should never be visible in haiku. There's a saying that the finger pointing to the moon is not the subject; the moon is.

Senyru – a haiku-like poem about people.

Haibun – a prose poem with one or more haiku/senyru attached.

Ode – A formal, often ceremonious lyric poem that addresses and often celebrates a person, place, thing, or idea. Its stanza forms vary.

The Wufflegrot – I invented this character for a bit of fun. My friend Jude in turn invented the Coet.

Table of Contents

Wufflegrot Series

A Small Explanatory Poem

When assonance and random rhyme combine
within the gentle flow of speech,
there's a balanced, subtle chime,
a whispered unity
that seems to me
entirely poetry.

A Spanish Drunk

Before his morning-after starts to pound,
before he's isolated by the crowd
he claims the curb, his body bent around
an agony of song; he cries aloud
in passionate flamenco, ages old.
His voice is patinated cobblestones
and honey-leather saddles glowing gold,
his voice is aching muscles, crumbled bones.
It translates somewhere primal where I hide.
My breath is stopped. His ardour kindles flames
where ice has held me since my own love died
and flays me with the richness that he claims.
Ironically the poet in my head
will never understand a word he said.

A Sparrow's Perspective

A square of grass. Tall buildings cluster near,
geometries cut angles in the sky,
impinge their frowning shadows, and yet here
a sparrow bathes in dust. He cocks his eye
at me a moment, then resumes his bath;
he fluffs his powder-puff of breast, it's pressed
into the hollow he has made. I laugh
to see him so intently focussed, blessed
with just a sparrow brain and powderings
to keep him happy. People hurry past
absorbed and stiff with stressful human things…
I sigh. For even buildings will not last;
they fall away to ruin, stones and rust.
Yet here a little sparrow bathes in dust.

Ah Keow and the Piglet – for Travis

It's our last day in Singapore.
Ah Keow has brought a baby pig.
It's very small and sleepy, and I crouch
to watch it feather-breathing snuffs of straw
that cling to moisture on its snout.
Poor little suckle-thing,
why has my servant brought you here,
sweating in a cardboard box
upon my kitchen floor?

We have to leave;
a truck is idling underneath our house and
loading all the sundry things we have to leave.

It's our last day in Singapore,
Ah Keow has got my baby son,
his fluffy auburn hair is sweated to her arm.
He has the lucky mark, a cherry spot;
she says that it's an ancient Chinese charm –
his eyes are blackest coal,
so she can see with certainty
his soul's Chinese.

We have to leave;
a truck is idling underneath our house and
loading all the sundry things we have to leave.

It's our last day in Singapore.
Leaving is an agony, it's like a little death,
the air is tight with grieving, bright with pain
but there's a kind of furtive eagerness that
makes me hold my breath,
what is it? Something... there it is again
something only out of sight
that I must see.

We have to leave;
a truck is idling underneath our house and
loading all the sundry things we have to leave.

Ah Keow has got my son,
a piglet's on my floor,
her husband waits within the truck
idling underneath our house and we must leave...
She holds him.
I demand my son.
She moves away.
I snatch my baby wordlessly,
I push her.
And I run.

Alas, Fair Knight – for Geoff Sanderson

Alas, fair knight, don't be deceived, for I
am such a friendly dragon. Here I lie
alone and sad, my freckled nose tucked in
between my paws. I turn and turn again;
the sun runs singing up and down my scales,
a rainbow scintillation shimmers high
into the atmosphere to catch the eye
of anyone who might appreciate
a beast like me. It seems to be a sin
to be a creature fabulous as sky,
but mister, I must tell you it's a bind
and multi-spangled beings ever cry
for company. It's always been our fate,
and listen mate, just don't believe the tales
you hear about us. See? We're really kind.
Yer; Dragon-kind, ha ha. Essentially
we're helpless Sir. We're brilliant. It's a shame.
So won't you be my friend? I'm not to blame.

Altruism

He flicked his lights at me when driving past,
to warn me that the cops were up ahead.
I checked the speedo, yes a little fast
so dropped it back. I thanked him in my head
and wondered why the driver was so kind,
for there's a risk in flashing lights this way;
I might have also been the 'fuzz'. My mind
began to drift back to another day…
recalling kids' recalcitrance. So then
is this a relic, does the child rebel,
or is it instinct gained from way back when
Cro-Magnon was the duty sentinel
who saved us from the lion in the grass?
I flick my lights to others as I pass.

Bedside Vigil

I sit and hold her hand as night draws in. Crickets call, a bat lands clumsily outside the window, in the tulip tree. A siren like a bird laments from far away.

curlew cry
an ambulance maps the streets
with sound.

She is dying. I watch her journey into the silent land. Her pulse falters. Moonlight flickers shadows on the eaves.

She has a plain gold wedding ring which has worn a little ridge into her finger. Her hand is soft but firm, the nails well-tended, the pads on her palm developed from constant work There is a scar there, by her little finger, the silky tether of it long healed, but drawing up the flesh to a tender pucker.

Beyond the circle of lamp-light, images form… I see her peeling vegetables, basting a roast on a cold winter night. Light shines along the carving knife. The kitchen is warm, voices swirl around her, plates and people wait for service. Blood spills beneath the tap, spirals around the plughole like a galaxy.

Children splash in soapy water, their squirming bodies shine. The air is humid, bubbles burst with scents of summer flowers. She hefts each child efficiently, towels them dry with practiced ease, dresses them in fresh pyjamas.

Now in dappled morning, brushing shiny tangled hair. She fastens ribbons, holds the little head to her chest, then lifts the glowing face to her own, cups rosy cheeks lovingly.
Her strong brown hands. They have wiped small noses and bottoms, bandaged hurts, mopped tears from flooding tragedy.

In this quiet room, her breathing changes. Small sighs are interspersed with long pauses. Blue shadows tint her nails.

A chilly wind begins to whisper in the reeds.

Rain splatters the window, and under another lamp-light a woman knits, the bright wool cascading over nimble fingers, softly growing heavy under them, each row building memory into fabric.

There's a film of sweat on her face. I sponge it gently away.

She's washing with a scrubbing board, bent over the sink, her hair damp with steam from the boiler, her face and hands red. There she is, standing tip-toe, her water-wrinkled fingers cool as they hang linen on a prop-held line, and later, she brings it in, tossing pegs into a tin bath, folds each item deftly.

Her dark hair spills across the pillow. They placed a red rose there.

Did these hands tend gardens? Did they gather flowers, arrange them carefully and place them where they would bring their stored sunshine to her world?

And now, beneath my own, winter creeps into her fingers... It is over. Her family couldn't bear to stay, but they wait, huddled together for warmth, at home.

autumn leaves
cluster shaking
in the cold wind.

I rise and call her family. I am so sorry.
It's Mother's Day.

Best Wishes

G'morning love. I've sent the dog to keep
you company. You always loved him, so
I'm all agog to think you'll meet! He'll leap
around in staggers, hobbled by the show
of happiness encoded in his tail,
and you'll be absolutely stoked to see
him there. So darling, here he is. Avail
yourself of him with lots of love from me.
It's lonely here without you. Guv was good
for me, but well, you know how fierce he is
with other dogs? We always knew he could
be quite a hazard, right? There's been a tiz,
my love; he killed the neighbour's pup. That's how
he came to die. It's why he's with you now.

Betrayal

Well, hello Daisy,
I didn't bring no flowers for your grave
and I won't be comin' back no more,
after today.

I found your letters, Daisy.
They were hid away
in that oaken box beside our bed.
Glory box, now there's a joke;
you shared your glory box around,
didn't you, Day!

God help me, but I never knew,
and damn you Day,
It's clear that you were never true to me
the way I was to you.
You opened me to ridicule,
and now I'm nothing but a bloody fool
after all those years.

I never knew you Daisy,
our marriage was a flamin' lie;
for you had all them lovers,
even my brother Jim;
that's how I opened up them letters
Day, when I seen that one from him.

And what about the children Daisy?
Are any of them mine?
I can't believe you done this
awful thing to them and me!
I put them ruddy letters

where the sun will never shine
and where the kids will never see.
I burnt the bloody lot.

So hello and goodbye, my dear,
I'll cry you no more tears,
I won't be comin' back no more,
after all these years.

Brisbane at Nightfall

As dusk approaches, gulls have gathered here
behind a fishing boat, their bodies white
and shining as they glide before the sheer
metallic-coloured river banks. Tonight
they'll rest upon the quiet waters, drift
in silence like the Lady of Shalott.
The city holds its breath. Now there's a shift
of light, pre-night is palest apricot…
and there against the backdrop of the sky
the flying foxes lift upon the air.
The pulsing of their wings as they go by
has quickened every heartbeat. Everywhere
above us sooty shapes whirl ever higher,
like bits of blackened paper from a fire.

By Jude-light

Our Jude said she is like a garden light,
that sheds a gentle, mellow glow.
Indeed, I see that this is so,
for I can see her standing firm, upright
in darkness, showing people where to go.
(Ho ho) But she
is like a lovely guiding light to me.

'Twas she who set my rambling, shambling feet
upon a metered path, she lit
my way, and now, because of it,
my poems run and play in measured beat.
And like a garden light, she does emit
(a bit) of cheer,
and I am always happy, when she's near.

Cause and Effect

A thorn that lodges deep will not reveal
the tethered scars within that hold it fast;
a wound inflicted never quite to heal
until the cause is taken out at last.
A woman cries in outrage at a wrong
for deeds whose hurt began long years ago
but locked away, the problems never solved
were hidden so that only she would know.
But now it festers, now her pain is strong;
her anger and her futile grieving tears
have grown to fury quite beyond control
from longing she's suppressed for fifty years.
She never learned to cope, she never will;
the thorn within her tissues festers still.

Cigs (gotta give 'em up)

They makes ya hoarse
they makes ya wheeze
and every time ya corfs
ya pees
but even tho they makes ya fret
you bet
ya wannanother cigarette.

They makes ya smell
they makes ya broke
they gives ya cancer
then ya croak
but even when ya life's a dag
a slag
ya reallywannanother fag.

They stunts ya growth,
they makes ya fart.
They rune ya figger
and ya heart
but even when ya feels it fail
tho pale
ya grabsanother coffin nail.

Comings and Goings

This still familiar road I drive again,
though years have passed and time has trimmed my mind,
reminders of the life we left behind
are sleeping here in landmarks that remain.
I park and walk the path my children ran,
beside the rocky creek that looks the same
as when we lived across the road, reclaim
the special feeling of this place. I scan
the land and find the hollow where we found
a broken nest of native mice, and here
we let them go when they were grown. Do you
my sons, recall our happy days around
this creek? The water is still bright and clear
but you are gone like mice, as children do.

Conned!

Kitty jumped onto my knee,
curled into a ball and purred,

tender feelings welled in me,
love or something like it stirred;
this small creature chose my lap!
Watch her take a little nap!
Curious I tried a test,
leant and turned the heater on,
what was warmest was the best,
presently the cat was gone!

How bemused I was to see
kitty jumping off my knee!

Country Fields

Here's the country where we ran

barefoot on the cattle pocked, flock mapped
rutted gutter tracks around the rounded hills,
down across the drenched grass
to the stream,

where fractured rainbows fizz and frisk
lamb-lively, silver spangled,
slipping ripple – sibilant between the trees.

Oh to be a child again.

Critical

Recrimination leaps from hiding
deep within.
My ego fights, denying fault.

But truth is bright as blood
in grasses lit with sun.

Dappled Leaf

When summer shadows write a song of trees
upon their dappled hieroglyphic grain
with sunlight semaphores of warming leaves
and supple branches fat with living rain,
their rhythms weave a pattern into time
as ancient as a fossil-fly in stone;
I reach with joy and claim the moment mine,
forever locked in amber, ever known.
The planet sings of life in rhythms slow
as eons and in music fast as light;
we feel the beat as seasons come and go
and subtle pulses flow with day and night.
And on the edge of chaos, patterns run
like shadows made of trees conducting sun.

Deep in Shade

My path is wild,
I breathe the Benedictine
notes of home,
branches taste my blood,
the rock my feet,
I unbecome again
reborn to earth.

Fantails woo my every move,
feather flirting air,
dancing insects from my step,
with cork-on-bottle cries.

The punga forest smell is
pungent, brown as dung,
familiar as the birthmark on my knee,
flaring hula skirts
about their kiwi-feather heart
curled and tender,
dreaming green;
concentric punkahs filter sun
their fronded thatch upon the earth
decays in damp embrace.

From the kowhai's harlot blooms
of bird-shaped daffodils
a tui drops a gleaming sound cascade,
rising at the end to pierce the heart,
repeated with a higher shard
and then a replicated cry of wood on wood,
the kiss of branches rich with rain.

Hiding underneath
reflections
a dappled eel of tiki green
sluices secretly,
its languid tail caresses,
mixing shadow tinctures,
cruising silent as a smile.

Deep in shade,
an eel, a bird,
I vanish
from myself.

Dinner's Served

We sit around the table. Mother brings
the meal, and we begin to eat, as clouds
of moths arrive to wing in spirals, fling
their bodies at the light, where they collide
to flutter stunned onto the tablecloth.

A moth has landed in the gravy, where
it struggles desperately before it drowns
and spreads a milky stain from sodden scales.
The youngest child lets out a wail, "Oh no!
A moth is in my food. How can I eat!"

But Father scoffs, says "Moths won't kill you son,
for they're a staple meal for some, look here."
He snatches rapidly and captures one
fat bodied, flapping, dazed unfortunate,
and stuffs it in his mouth. We watch, amazed.

The moment's led the man and moth into
a trap, and in a trice it dawns on him,
the trap is his big silly gob. A blob
of mothy-stuff is on his tongue, his eyes
go wide; he feels that wriggle there inside.

And then we laugh. He has to swallow now
and when he does we lean back in our chairs
to gasp for air, collapse in helpless mirth,
and brush our tears away with shaking hands.
But Travis ate his meal, and now, though years
have gone, when moths fly round that time of year
we smile and call, "Hey Peter! Dinner's here."

The Dog and I

The dog and I went walking
jaunty in the morning,
sunshine lemon light.

I had him on a tight lead
but he dragged me to a fence and bit a dog there on the other side.
He got it by the lip and would not let go.
He shook his head.
Blood flew.

I yelled commands and pulled his choker chain
to no avail,
dogs screamed and scrambled.
People came.

The owner tried to pry their mouths apart
he yelled to others "Get the hose!"

A man came running from across the road and he hit my dog hard
with a piece of wood
across the nose
hard
very hard.

He let go.

The owner of the dog shouted at me
"I want your name
and your address.
You will pay for this.

You want to do something about that dog, lady."

He ran inside his yard.

I waited
leaning on another fence
all heartbeat

spinning
breathless
sweating

blood dripped from my dog's mouth.
he hung his head.

People watched.

(Gates and windows owned their people
tin soldiers stiff and cold.
Sentries standing post,
little leaden groups.)

I waited
leaned
and breathed
blood dripped

A car stopped
"Are you all right?"
"Did they hit your dog?"

The owner strode towards me yelling,
spitting hatred.
"My dog's hurt!"

"I want your name!"
"Don't you walk away!"

His body big
and tight
his features twisted
snarling
shouting
loud
loud

"I want your name!
you'll pay!"

My voice like a shadow
"I'm prepared to be reasonable sir
don't walk away…"
but he turned his back again.

Blood dripped.

I'm so alone.

I stumbled home.

The dog is out the back
where he will stay.

What can I say?
I go back
cheque book in my hand
His dog is honey-golden warm

and licking at the gate
just a scratch there on his velvet nose.

His master's drinking with his mate
out on the porch
of the house
across the road.
"My dog is fine," he says,
and nothing more.

Dogfight

I can't forget the power of his will
through the lead
when I was tethered
to his urge to kill

and helpless
in the teeth of it.

Dreams of Better Days

The wind is bitter here. It blows the snow
that gathers in this ruined castle's keep,
in frozen empty rooms. On rocks below,
it's blackened talus groans before the deep
where leaping torrents lash and surge. A cry
as though long-tortured phantoms woke from sleep
goes winding round the ramparts, howling high
without a pause... The might and dreams of men
are shattered here; forgotten remnants lie
in rust of broken swords and faded pen-
marks in abandoned tomes. These walls withstood
the ravages of men, but now again
they hurry back to stone, where creatures hide
and books returned to wood await the tide.

Enjoying Destroying Nature

The ocean called his name, the simple heart
of him. He came, deep breathed the pristine air
in great long sighs, and closed his eyes... the dart
of sharp-finned stresses slowed and drifted, there
on inner tides, and when he walked, at peace,
along the long, long stretch of untouched sand,
the gentle waters lapped his feet in cease-
less warm caress. He lit a smoke and scanned
the endless sparkle blending into sky,
contemplatively quaffed another beer,
then threw the empty bottle, arced it high
to glisten amber light. It splashed down near
another. What a great trajectory!
Relaxed, content, he pissed into the sea.

Equestrian Blomquestrian

(A joke presented as a sonnet, invented by Eric Bloomquest)

A woman strode into the clubhouse bar
and stood there solidly, her legs apart,
her jodhpurs sticking out a bit too far.
She waited by the cafe á la carte
deciding that she'd stay to have a bite
(when she'd dispatched a foaming stout or two)
because she had a way to ride that night.
She shifted restlessly from shoe to shoe.
But no one came to offer her a drink;
the staff were watching footy out the back
to rowdy cheers and she began to think
they'd never show. At last came barman Jack;
"You waiting to be served?" we heard him say.
"Oh no," she said, "I always stand this way."

Evil Energy Roils In Me

At first I ran trailing electricity
my hair on fire
but it helped me do the things I had to do
when letting him down was not an option.

Later I let it drive me to diversions;
anything to fill the days
without him.

Then here with my parents, day by boring day
the energy had to be stilled... quieter quieter until
panic trilled in my legs
fizzed, flushed and burned
coiled inside.

I missed him even more for having nothing to do
except miss him in everything.

Then cried for the loss of him to comfort me,
cried for his loss of me
and the world

his precious energy gone gone gone

The thing is, suppressing this panic energy has made me afraid;
afraid to risk moving for the immensity of his loss
releasing that which is his loss

trapped inside even as I am trapped
inside this house, inside
my obligations, duty,
and love

but now,
because my son has called me
the energy screams in my legs, shrieks down my spine
pulls me gasping over hills dank with leaves
green as only my land is green, rich with memories
and his eyes looking through mine
his voice his smile his love
inside the gaping hole he left

but warm and painful in my loving of him still

I will go to see our sons
and let the evil energy
run free.

Fairies at the Bottom of the Garden

At dawn, when sunshine spills across the grass,
my eye is drawn to fuzzy balls of light
that float and flit on gauzy wings. They pass
down low to skim the dandelions, their flight
controlled, describing angles as they go
criss-crossing rapidly without a pause
so that it's hard to see them clearly, though
here's one that hovers near, defying laws
of physics… Oh, it's just a dragonfly.
A pity, for I thought I'd seen the dance
of sylvan sprites. Ah, Mother Nature's sly,
for where there's prey there'll always be a chance,
and here's a tic-tac-toe of silver webs
to catch the morning fairies by the legs.

Fall of a Sparrow

The sparrow trembles in my hand. He's cold,
his feathers wet, bedraggled by the storm
that threw him down so savagely. I hold
him close, inside my coat to keep him warm.

How frail we are, this bird and I! The flame
that fires the atom drives the smallest cell,
but there's a greater mystery. Its name
is life. It's precious, we protect it well.

We reach a hut. At last my fears subside.
We sleep, though faith and logic rage outside.

Fog

We walk to school in fog that seems to wait for us,
motionless and silent.
It clears a space as we walk into it,
closes again behind,
a disturbed slipstream moving in slow motion.
We inhale slow illustrated eddies,
exhale sudden fountains that escape to cool
and drop away disappointed,
we hold the breath of fog within us like a secret,
become fog, blind and silent.

We listen for muted sounds
of cattle drumming on the road;
they're suddenly here snorting, steaming curls,
flanked by sheeted clouds,
their faces demons ghost-grey-on-black,
their lumbering bodies reckless
and we run to find a cattle-shelter
white on white,
safety in the snail-shell centre.
The beasts go by filling the air with stink,
shaking worlds as our hearts thunder
and the fog closes us together
like a Christmas diorama in a jar.

Down by the river the kuia gather,
scarves about their heads, huddled
in long dark dresses,
outlines smudged, merged into the grey.
Fog mourns about the river, rises
to blur features, but their moko
move blackly, bobbing as they speak,

voices humming in warm layers.
They look like phantoms, and now

when I recall them there
they have become wraiths in fact,
lost like mist itself...

kuia – grandmother
moko – chin tattoo

Forgive – rondeau redoublé for Travis

Forgive yourself, my son, for errors past,
for weaknesses are only strengths reflected;
mistakes that seem so glaring, when recast
may bring solutions if they are respected.

Adventures led to outcomes unexpected;
and some were bound to leave you quite aghast,
in light of reason, do not be dejected,
forgive yourself, my son, for errors past.

Oh hold your self-respect and hold it fast!
Your tender heart deserves to be protected,
and self-recrimination cannot last,
for weaknesses are only strengths reflected.

Your strengths are vital, let them be directed,
for deep within you lies a wisdom vast;
you'll see how inexperience affected
mistakes that seem so glaring, when recast.

And when the benefits you have amassed,
when all the stepping-stones have been connected,
be proud my son that journeys unsurpassed
may bring solutions if they are respected.

Then when your future course has been selected,
please know that strengths and weaknesses contrast;
they complement each other when inspected,
there never was a need to be downcast.
Forgive yourself my son.

Friends

We saunter casually, in dappled shade,
towards the river. Branches gently sway.
A bird cries gleaming sounds… they glide, cascade
like threaded bubbles spilling down to spray
the air with silver. Sunlight sparkles tease
our eyes from water glimpsed beyond the rise:
it slides with slinking waves, wee vortices.
We sit and talk of friends, we empathise
with flowing warmth. We share our poetry,
and laughter comes as simply as our heart-
beats, in companionship and bonhomie.
The hours fly. It's time for us to part.
Today's the first time we have ever met.
We got to know each other on the Net.

Frogs' Water Voices

Rain falls...
water voices call,
each from a hidden place
like secrets revealed.
Soft leather throats
sing their world
with bell-sounds drowned,
in wind-chimes licked and tasted.

They ring
in simple exclamations that burst
like brittle bubbles,
brilliant tones demand
in shards of glass
that spear the air with urgency.
Frog-voices cry
of mating in their element with joy,
of buoyancy and plunge,
in waters made of sky.

They chant concentric pulses:
"Come to me."
Caressing over surface-tension...
percussion buffeting so
sensuous to skin,
and to waiting organs
chiming deep within.

"Know the silky kiss of water lapping
velvet vents vibrating with my song,
of water eggs that bubble free,
electric slip and slide,
fierce grip and kick;
O moot it be!"

Rain falls...
water voices call.

Grandad's Diary

A butterfly lay sleeping like a princess in a spell,
inside its caterpillar skin that, hardened to a shell,
became a package full of magic, full of mystery.
It hung beneath a leaf, a lovely thing to see, and Bree
was certain it would please her grandad, when he wasn't well.

And so the parcel came. The chrysalis inside its cell-
like jar delighted him, for Bree's amazing gift to tell
him he was loved meant he could share in her discovery:
a butterfly.

He watched it split its shell and climb, a living jewel, to swell
its wings. They glittered in the sun. He saw a parallel
between the shining insect and the soul, for both are free,
and later, both went winging high to seek their destiny.

Amazingly we saw outside the door, to say farewell:
a butterfly.

Haibun for Jude

Her funeral today. At this hour those who love her meet to say goodbye. Not only there in Dubbo, with her family, but in quiet places right around the world.

We knew her on the internet and so it's fitting that together, far apart, we hold her in our hearts here in this Sky-Wide Church.

A bird drops a long feather. It spirals, wafts, settles without a sound. I remember how I wrote a note to her on paperbark, using a sharpened quill, because she loved all of life and birds especially.
She still had it last month.

That's when we met for the first time. She was as I knew her. On the internet, via poetry, knowing comes from a deeper level.

I think about the way the sea reflects the sky, so it goes right to the edge of it and back, and then exchanges itself with it, in a cycle. Sea to sky, as evaporation, back again as rainfall, round and round, like the tides, like life... some say that there is reincarnation too.

Goodbye my friend.

Like the ocean to the shore, I will return here, as my memories turn and turn again.

sky wide
and back again –
the sea.

Heel in the Dust

Summertime;
barefoot we squat in the dust,
heat on our shoulders,
sweaty hair tendrils plastered to our faces.
We breathe each other's breath;
sweetish smell of hot children.

Summer heat and dust,
cicada song percusses
an exciting
background.
We are united, together on this day
lost in time
intent on marbles.

Heel in the dust!
Twirl. Behold!
Magic circle!
Colosseum for our game,
marbles the players,
each a star
placed in concentric orbits
like the cosmos.
We the Gods
deflecting, deciding their fate.

Who will own them, hold them to the light,
marvel on their beauty?
Ownership. Victory.
Drop them in the bag!
Oh the clink! The chink!
The summertime sound of
marbles.

I grow skillful
coveting marbles.
Heavy steelies forged in flame,
metal smooth
boneys creamy white,
silky on my tongue.

Marbles!
Dreams caught in light
lights caught in dreams,
each a wonder
like a fly in amber.

They are mine and I am theirs.
Here in this time.

Here comes Father in his prickly railway clothes.
Big, gruff Father with his deep loud voice.
"Little girls do not play marbles!"
"But, Daddy, I do!"
"Not any more you don't!"
He takes my marbles, gives them to my brothers.

I grieve.
It makes no sense.

I find a marble peacock blue;
it winks at me from
under the dresser.
Defiant, I win back my marbles.
Back from the neighbourhood boys,
back from my brothers.

Then I play no more.

Hidden Things

This morning's rosy dawn has warmed the sand,
a sea-bird holds the air; its feathers blush
with sky. Cool tones fold into warmth, it lands
where lilac ripples underlie the rush
of gentle surges on the shore. The tide
is out. The beach is hushed, a little boat
lies nodding, bobbing, sleeping on its side.
A filigree of lacy bubbles floats
a moment, then is gone. The sea-bird strikes
down viciously – it knows where molluscs live:
their tiny breaths betray them. Now he spikes
them in his bill. He takes what nature gives.
I gasp for tender things I'll never tell...
in silence, secrets live inside my shell.

Hogmanay – for Barry

December closing in to Hogmanay…
to voices whisky moist and harsh with smoke,
as laughter spittled exclamations pound
the air. It's hot, and boxed inside the batch
we jostle, hidden rancours crackle. Games
in progress flare with busy skirts. They watch,
manoeuvre slyly in the ancient way
that women do.

I seek a quiet place to feed my son,
away from thick electric air and sound;
my body builds him strong against the world,
against the years he'll have to fight alone.
In peace we hold the turbulence away,
we fold a cloak of privacy around
us and we sway in crooning privacy.
Our time is short.

December closing down on Hogmanay.
In heavy heat this humid night, the brittle
clink of glasses; spirits warmed in bodies
rise to vaporise and clothes are wringing
in the ringing air. With bellowed laughter,
yells and squealed cries, hungry egos press
for light. In veiled glances messages
unspoken, fly.

"It's time you weaned that baby, by the way.
Or will you suckle him forever? There's
a point where decency is past, you know.
My sons were fed on bottle milk, and they
are strong as anyone. And what is more,

I think that you are starving him. All for
the sake of show."

The baby's crying in the raucous fray,
I gather him, a tender bundle, to
my breast. He nestles hungrily, but heat
and stress combine to steal his nourishment
away, for all too soon the milk is spent.
I hear the self-fulfilling prophecy
and now it is essential that I rest.
I kiss his head.

December closes in on Hogmanay...
now I must drink a river, I must sleep,
yet bidden stay to see the New Year in;
my obligation to the family
holds sway, my protestations fade away
to celebration and the black-haired man
who brings the coal in through the midnight door.
As all first-foot the year in revelry,
Time's babe is born.

The family is reeling, thumping on
the wooden floor. I hold my son
and grieve; my milk has vanished with the year.
Alone I tell my failure to the dawn,
I weep for he who grew his life from mine,
for intimacy lost, for sharing gone,
along with trust. I'm just a pawn in some
old female game.

Hokkien Halloween

Singapore in the fifteen-minute dusk
down Meng Suan road
moated by monsoon drains.
People hurry home,
chased by long grey shadows.

Tonight
no one sits smoking on the pavement.
The street is empty.
Tonight, shut inside,
they watch for Hungry Ghosts,
not looking, in case they see.

I walk
hushed, expectant,
eager for the lurch,
the shambling gait, the flash and
flit of spirits
freed this night.

But there are none.
They do not come.
Homely altars
smoke thin streams of incense
to curl above dishes of fish,
and rice, of fruit-filled bowls
for the ghosts.

Chiming voices murmur
Chinese prayers,
silent streams, spirit-song;
deftly burnt paper money

carries to spirit hands
ethereal as smoke.

The altars are still there next morning,
no ghost tore at the food with ghastly teeth,
nor even nibbled daintily.
The fruit, the fish, the rice is there,
the incense underneath.

They did not come.
Not even one.

I'm Bloody Glad You're Dead, Kym

I'm bloody glad you're dead, Kym,
before the summer rain
could bring you storms to make you shake
and run, to dribble pee across the floor again,
before the fireworks quaked your wonky pins
and filled your dim old nose.
They always made your face go tight
and wrinkled up in rictus. Yes I'm glad that those
damn frights of smoke and light
and blasted sound won't reach you where you lie.
I thought you'd die last year on Guy Fawkes day,
or that the summer sun would do you in.
I'm bloody glad you're dead, Kym.
This season would have killed you anyway.

Impermanence

The world is just the same; sunlight sparkles
on the leaves and I remember
climbing trees like these;
I dropped a cat to see her land
as they're supposed to do.

She broke her leg and just as
then I hide above and close
my eyes now tragedy
is underneath.

Stones and dirt and wood the bones
and broken flesh of Earth
from which we build our houses
till they fall
and rain comes

in

tender
light on mist your breath
slows down.
Water drips to chill my spine but
I can turn to catch you still,
to hold your hand and kiss your brow,
my fierce familiar love for you
unchanged

forever

till I fall.

Jackie

That little fellow, Jack, can hardly wait.
He'll soon be five, he'll walk with us to school;
each day he waits for us, "See ya" he says
and waves, he lifts his brows and tilts his head
in Polynesian style, he is so sweet!

Jackie little Jackie-down-the-street.

The men are in the river side by side,
their bodies bright with sparkles as they wade
a long slow march, the ripples dance and shine,
and no one speaks, I watch the shadows grow,
until they reach like fingers that would hide,

down inside the river by the pipe.

There's an awful cry, and one man stoops
and snatches, boiling up the water where
a child comes swinging out in fountain gouts
that stream in rivers down his little arms
spread out like Jesus' arms upon the cross.

Jackie, little Jackie-down-the-street.

Then suddenly the air is full of sound;
the women on the bridge let out a wail
that's crying on and on and I can see
the shape of it go spreading like a stain,
I see it beating like a wounded gull

flying up the river past the pipe.

Now Jackie's on the claypan by the bank,
his father sucks his mouth and spits a flood.
We stand and watch him press on Jackie's chest
and darkness grows around, we breathe the cold,
but Jackie doesn't breathe, he doesn't move.

Jackie little Jackie-down-the-street.

Doc Tommo's car spins arcing in a skid;
he runs and kneels, he fingers Jackie's throat
and looks into his eyes. "It's way too late,"
the doctor says, "Give up, it's over Sid,
give up I said! He's dead! He's bloody dead!"

Jackie little Jackie-down-the-street.

His father picks him up in his big arms
and holds him close against him wordlessly.
We watch him trudging slowly up the hill,
and Jackie's mother follows heavily,
and everything is still now as I sit

down above the river on the pipe

where Jackie fell and hit his head. He sank
but no one said a thing – they ran away
because they got a fright. Oh how I wish
we never took him with us after school
to fish, and play the way he did today,

half across the river on the pipe.

Journey – for Matt

We made a collage,
precious tokens from this time together;
fragments of rock, seeds, shells, feathers
cupped in a scapula, symbols
of creation, regeneration, seachanges.

Found,
treasures of the Earth and of the spirit;
a son long lost, a mother.
Small steps over rough terrain but
I could not reach you
cloistered in the ramparts of yourself,
shielded against everyday spears
which lancinated, made you bleed.

Travailing sensitivity drove you
to inner caverns
where intuition gathers,
where deeper meanings illuminate
and protect.

Time stilled.
I reached blindly,
touched you at last,
warm and hushed with focussed intensity,
as you were the day
you were gifted to me
from the universe, through my body.

On our last day
you knelt to contemplate
the essence we captured

in found treasures;
my heart caught with love for you,
my tears salted your hair.

Small tokens
of moments in time,
new beginnings, rainbows.
Found treasures
cupped in a scapula;
elements of Earth,
energies reborn.

Remember our journey, know my truth.
I hold you in my heart.
Your life is your own, but I am your mother.
Remember I love you
forever.

Journey at a Trot

I'm very busy now. I'm scaling heights,
I'm swimming after dark from winter shores;
the fishers know my name, and there are nights
when ragged people warm my heart, because
they share the little that they have. I've slept
upon the beach, sung jazz up on the stage,
and wandered wild for days where sorrow crept
to snuffle at my heels. I know the cage
that is my isolation. Here's the door.
Just watch me run! I gasp, my body aches
but still I must go on, there must be more!
I'll find the energy although it takes
Its toll of me. My love has passed away.
I push to just get through another day.

Just Coping

Tommy Thomkins likes his biscuits
black with beer,
when he's full of blackish biscuits,
Tommy has no fear.
Tommy knows a world of strangers
is a scary place,
here comes Tommy, blythe and happy;
Tommy's off his face.

Layers

What secrets lie behind your eyes, my love?
What anguish do you try to hide from me?
Is Vietnam still burning there,
where children's voices cry?
Where violence strips the living meat from men
in memory?

What dreaming keeps the sleep from you, my love?
What makes your anger rise without a cause?
You've kept it back away from me,
not shown it, but I've known it
coiling, roiling deep and dark in you

these many years;

the napalm dragon
with the common people in its jaws.

Lim Ah Im and the Snake

Lim Ah Im is crying,
cradling her swollen hand.
She thinks a snake is underneath the skin.
She tells me that the snake will die;
the Chinese doctor burnt some herbs:
little pyres, little fires
to kill the snake within.

I sit beside her on the sofa.
"Oh Im-ah, Lim Ah Im,
we of the west have much to learn
from Chinese medicine
but we would call your snake another name,
we would say a germ has gotten in;
the red line is your body fighting.
Let us help it win.

Im-Ah, it is difficult for me,
but this is like Mah Jong,
like burning joss sticks
to the god of fortune, Top-he Kong;
we can make our chances double
two times (ched, nung)
come to my western doctor
to make your body strong
and then we'll stop and say Ja ba boh
and make fires for Top-he Kong."

Literacy in Noodles

Lim Ah Im, (in English, Kim,)
Im-ah when we were friends,
couldn't read or write,
not in Chinese nor in any other way.
I was amazed.
Here is your name. I show her.
KIM.
LIM AH IM.
I write it big for her to copy
and I sound each letter out;

"Each one makes your name, you see."
She laughs,
"That be my name?
It look like mee!"
"Like me? Chinese noodles, oh,"
I look again;
strands upon the paper;
gentle loops.
"Oh, Im-Ah!
It looks like that to you?
Oh, ha ha!
So it does!
And my name too."

Lofty Aspirations – for Matt

You climb. The unforgiving rock beneath
your body summons all your strength of mind
and muscle, all your skill. Here in the teeth
of pure survival, doubt is left behind;
each vivid moment slices the mundane
away, reveals a crystal of the true.
You live by your decisions, find the vein
of courage deep inside, your focused view.
The summit's near, a rim against the sky.
You dole a rope out from the belt that girds
your waist, attach it to pitons, apply
a final effort, find at last what words
cannot express. The highest. Effort paid.
Your pain, handmarked in chalk, already fades.

Luthur, Flying Fox, Foster Child

He tumbled out of night as black as he;
his family to mine. His mother cried
and flew away, a shadow ebony
against the moon. He'd snuggle safe inside
his water-bottle bed where, warm and fed,
he'd sleep enfolded, sucking on his wrap,
a baby upside down. Inside his head
he had a map: he'd swim the floor, or flap
around the house to find us. He would cling
so close, click-purring, swinging rhythmically,
and later, when we'd walk in night, he'd wing
from trees to me. Of course, we set him free,
but now, when black-on-black folk, all the same,
percuss the night with wings, I call his name.

Memories of a Maungaturoto Childhood

Tiny railway settlement adjacent to the line,
twenty little houses all of similar design.
Some of them were only huts and some were further back,
twelve were clustered side by side around a metal track.

Lost in lovely farming land, the station served the town,
miles away from where we ran as free as thistle down.
Leather-hard our naked feet were hardly ever still;
country beckoned all around us and we roamed at will.

Sledging down a hillside summer roasted hard and dry!
Kites with ribs of bracken fern escaping to the sky!
Hopscotch and cats-cradle, games of skipping, knuckle-bone.
Fishing streams with signatures of perfume all their own.

Bicycles and trolleys, scooters, stilts and pogo sticks,
football, cricket, baby animals and fluffy chicks,
"Go Home Stay Home," "Magic Glue," and Chasey in the dark,
public bonfires, burn the Guy to watch him smoke and spark!

Huts up in the tree-tops tall and huts in scrub and fern,
wanderings in native bush till twilight bade return,
children of New Zealand irrespective of our race,
brought together for a heart-beat in a magic place.

In my mind the best of times were spent there on the land;
living close to nature there is much to understand.
From that time we learned respect for every living thing
and the peace companionship and harmony can bring.

Minnie

"Come sit upon my bed, I want to ask
you for a favour when my soul is free.
Though this may seem to be a petty task
to you, it means an awful lot to me.
When I have died, (it will be any day)
go to the Sally Army in my stead;
please take my clothes and give them all away.
Now, promise you will do this, when I'm dead."
But Minnie's clothing had designer tags
and others argued for them, so in fact
I had to stuff them into rubbish bags
and smuggle them away to keep our pact!
She'd left a present in the drawer below;
a diary for the year she'd never know.

Moon Festival

In memory I see my children's faces
flicker-dappled, candle bright,
holding swaying paper lanterns
borne on supple sticks.
From darkness all around us, muted mellow lights,
trailing plumes of curling smoke
evoked of tallow wicks;
fish and birds and animals come floating in the night
glowing magically like coloured phantoms
on the humid air.

Printed on the inside of my lids
I see the lanterns glow
from far and near in little groups
that move with careful slowness
as we go
over the bridge and through the Kampong
to the people of Nee Soon
'til all about are lanterns, lanterns, lovely lanterns
shining, shining like the moon!

Candlelight will ever make a recall spark
these special times, these gifts of things Chinese,
the busy streets, the laughter, gongs and Chinese chimes,
the easy joy and chatter in another place and time
when comradery's a lantern deep in dark.

My Dolly

My dolly's gone, I've lost her.
Do you think she ran away?
I was a bit unkind to her
just yesterday.

Though my Mummy growled at me.
It was dolly who was bad,
but my dolly kept on smiling
when I was sad.

I smacked her on the bottom,
really hard. I pulled her hair,
but that dolly kept on smiling.
She didn't care.

I growled at her like Mummy,
then I threw her in the drain.
I looked for her this morning though,
out in the rain.

And now I think I've lost her.
Now I think she's run away.
I was a bit unkind to her,
just yesterday.

My Heart is Like a Wellstream

My heart is like a wellstream
that sometimes seems to fail,
when not a drop of water can be found,
and I despair.
There's nothing there.
I have no welling love, just barren ground.
around the place it used to be. The seam
of rock has closed, the sparkling trail

gone dry. I have no feelings any more.

My heart is like a high tor
that's blown by bitter snows,
till suddenly the stone is thrown aside
when someone's pain
has touched again
the place where mercy grows, and opens wide
the crust that kept it deep inside. A pour
of fellow-feeling gushes, rushes, flows…

my heart is still a wellstream, as before.

Nana

She didn't believe in gambling
Thought it was a sin.

I loved her,
loved her familiar strange grimaces
and writhing movements,
her voice which would change pitch
like an adolescent boy's.
She was my Nana.

I went nursing
met a woman with strange grimaces
and writhing movements.
Huntington's Chorea.
St. Vitus' Dance.
Just like my Nana.

Nana had no choice.
She never knew
about the two-up game in her genes,
the 50/50 chance she dealt her children.
She didn't believe in gambling
Thought it was a sin.

Nanny Long

A witch lived in our street.
wrinkled and bent
just like the one in Hansel and Gretel.
We were afraid of her,
ran past her house
or crept up her pathway,
knocked on her door and ran away.
Serve her right for being a witch!

I had a bantam hen.
She was mine all mine.
Sit her on a ping-pong ball
she would lay a tiny egg
just my size.
Sit her on a clutch
she would go clucky.

Banty had four chicks
and me her surrogate
helping to find food for them.
Under boards, under rocks
Bok bok! Look, look!
Wings curved up, out,
bob bob, beak pointing
scratch X, X X,
Bok bok!
Show the chicks!

By the wood pile
railway sleepers compact
the soil heavily embedded.
What treasures will be there
underneath!

I pull. Banty waits.
So very heavy!
Moss-slippery.
At last, it lifts a bit a bit more.
The chickens run underneath.

"Run little chickies RUN!
I can't hold it! RUN!"

CHOCK!!
a lemon chick has caught a leg
pulls free, ricochets off to the ditch
moving horribly!

Where are the others oh no!

I run, screaming
"Mummy mummy come quickly!
The cat's got the chickens!
The cat's got the chickens no
no it didn't I squashed them o come!"

Flat.
Flat like my pressed flowers
flat
beaks all broken

eyes popped
and flat.
Legs out like drawings
burst and dead and
flat.
One in the ditch has a broken leg
and it suffers
I did it.

Mother makes me dig a grave
with the tablespoon.
I sob so hard I can hardly breathe,
I did it I did it I did it
I killed them!
I begin to vomit and it doesn't stop.

The Witch comes running
"What are you doing to that child!
I can hear her clear down the street!"
Mother is angry but smiles in a funny way.
"I'm punishing her. She killed the chickens"
"For heaven's sake woman!
Don't you think she's suffered enough!
Run inside now."
She finished the grave for me.

Next day when I lay listlessly
still vomiting,
she brought me a colouring book
and crayons
"Here you are, child.
It's a new day."

Not Our Fault

The chair has made us lazy,
oh no, it wasn't us;
how could we not be lazy,
it's luxurious!

The food has made us greedy,
we never chose to be;
it's meant to make us greedy,
for bonhomie!

The wine has made us drunken,
It's got nought to do with us;
It's made to make us drunk, an'
it's salubrious!

The years have made us hedonists,
it's how we have to live;
we never think we're hedonists;
we're appreciative!

Now and Then

But light a candle, watch them move again,
no longer merely paintings on the roofs
of Altamira Cave. A flying mane
flings scent, an arrow thuds, and clattered hooves
slide ringing here where palm-prints claim a home.
Though aeons changed the Spanish Pyrenees,
we empathise with those who used to roam
here, fighting bravely for their families.
These days I live my life with retrospect
and present time that drags slow feet to gaze
at images of us that leap, sun-flecked,
in children born to ours. Within the haze
that separates us now, I measure time
in happiness that once was yours and mine.

Nun With Roses

An aged nun arranges roses,
fervid face aglow;
gnarled fingers linger lovingly,
and gently stroke
silken petals curled and furled,
living velvet,
steeped in perfume.
Lovely, lovely!

Her lips move in prayer,
"Thank you God for these
thy gifts of beauty sent to please us."
She cups fat teardrop blooms
moist with dew,
each a benediction,
lifts them to her lips,
breathes a tactile sacrament,
sacred communion.

I smile to myself and wonder
what would she do
should she realise
she's caressing sex organs,
amputated to grace a vase.

Ode to a Lost Falcon

Beloved bright and beautiful, we mourn;
they say you fell. We hear they found you dead
this morning on a balcony, and torn
by flaying winds we weep for you who fed
on life as we do, helplessly. We saw
you born from falconshell, upon a ledge
of pebbles high within our city's heart,
where through a voyeurs' eye we watched you fledge.
And though we shivered at the way you tore
at life, we marvelled, loved you even more
for fierceness and skill, the killer's art.

Beloved bold and beautiful, we cry
for you. We empathise, for we who grasp
at life with passion, understand; we try
our eager wings against the wind, we clasp
the things we love so strongly, yet we take
the risk of crashing as we lift on air.
Oh fierce avian we say goodbye
in sadness; you were young. Our hearts will ache
in memory of you when falcons play.
We'll watch them plunge and wheel in joy; we'll say
it is for freedom that we live and die.

Ode to Courage (from a palliative care nurse)

Beyond the hope of seasons hidden deep
in time denied, beyond the aching reach
of outstretched fingers grasp, you ever keep
your dignity, oh Courage. Fate may bleach
our mortal bones, but in the turbulence
of living, it is you who testifies
to strength; you are the spirit's troubadour,
your song a quiet focus that defies
finality of death. Your evidence
inspires – it shows the soul's magnificence.
You live in memory for evermore.

Oh Aenid

Oh Aenid, how you sparkled, how you shone!
With blackest eyes that laughed with merriment!
Demeanour filled with charm and humour warm;
a lady from a famous family.

Oh Aenid, fate was cruel, so unkind!
Your fragile body held the gene to maim!
Relentlessly your brain flew all to sparks
and lightning ran unchecked to every nerve!

Oh Aenid, how I loved you to the end!
When restlessly your body writhed and jerked!
And all your wit and beauty turned to ugliness
your mindless dripping tongue upon your breast!

Oh Aenid, gracious beauty trapped inside!
How I wept to see you come to this!
For dignity, that precious thing, was gone.
A gargoyle held you suffering in thrall!

Oh Aenid, in your lineage I see
this evil happened time and time again!
Perhaps grand-uncle Humphry Davy tried
to find the answer to this mystery!

Oh Aenid, did he search to find a cure?
Was electricity a clue for him?
I read that Mary Shelley knew him well,
and he inspired the story Frankenstein!

Oh Aenid, other minds have not forgot!
The genome now is mapped, the end is near!
If only people steel themselves to act
your line from now 'til ever may be free!

Oh Mummy Come Quick!

I thought my mouse would scare the chooks,
I thought it would be fun to see them run
in panic from my mouse
underneath their house.
I thought of elephants, I'd heard they cried when they saw one
at least it said so in my books.

I pushed my mouse right under there,
it waddled slowly out onto the dirt.
I lay down flat to see
the chooks all squawk and flee;
a chook is such a dope, as if a fluffy mouse could hurt,
I thought that they would get a scare.

A chook came underneath the shed,
its feathers rose up on its scrawny neck.
It bent its head to look.
Oh what a silly chook.
I nearly laughed aloud to see that hen but it went PECK!
It pecked until my mouse was dead.

The chooks are underneath their house,
I am afraid of them, their beaks are wet.
I am a murderer
there's nothing left but fur
but how was I to know a chook would kill my little pet?
'cos it was just a furry mouse.

On the Verge

Alone. It's hot. Familiar odours steam
in tones of brown. The trees are breathing earth;
dark humus wets their feet and mine. I lean
against an ancient puriri, its girth
a measurement of time. It gathers me,
absorbs my consciousness, and gives me birth
into another world… of energy
that flows between the trees, that fiercely sweeps
in elemental chaos from the sea
and buffets, sneers at innocence that sleeps
upon the threshold. Help! A sly green man
is giggling in the leaves, enchantment creeps
in tangled vines. I run while yet I can,
my feet inspired by panic, lent by Pan.

Peetian (sonnet form invented by Judie Peet)

This woodland's lonely; lost and dry,
Australian as the she-oak cones
that lie in dust beneath our feet.
They're husked by cockatoos that fly
a haven where they've made their homes –
this dam that honours Judie Peet.
My friend, forever this is yours.
Your name is written on this sign;
custodian you were indeed.
We won't forget you, Jude, because
of glossy blacks whose feathers shine
as they come here to drink and feed.
I heard the glossies' wheezing cry
It's just as if they said goodbye.

Post Pandemic Cure (the Nose Dwellers)

Though constellations whirl beyond our home,
we live in perfect bliss,
for we, the Urg, are happy, safe, and warm.
Within this cave, a honeycomb
of narrow halls with vaulted walls
and cosy folds in which to laze;
we praise the God that led us all to this.

We wandered far to find this pleasant place,
through mighty winds that blew
and drew us, as by magic, up a face
to here, our blessed breathing-space.
We spend our days in joy, amazed;
we feast, we dance and sing, half-crazed
in worship of the Love that brought us through.

Then all at once, in incandescent light,
our God appeared! We rose
and ran to where He stood, too blazing bright
to see! We fell bedazzled by His might.

"Go back to bed," the doctor said,
and put his torch away. "I'll write
a script for you. Just squirt it up your nose."

Preserving Dignity

We find her crumpled on the floor at 2am.
Appalled, we do a quick assessment there, and then
I kneel and hold her, Patty goes to get a chair
and Tilly says, "Oh when you two have finished there
I'll have a bedpan."

We gently lift up Maudy working as a team
and wheel her to the loo where Pat elects to stay,
I run a pan to Tilly Brown, who says, "Oh, you
will never ever guess what I have done today,
I ate an ice-cream!"

Maudy's dying, Maudy has a fistula;
a vaginal track that seeps her blood and waste.
It breaks our hearts to find her fallen on the floor,
she tries so hard. And Tilly calls, "I'd like a taste
of a Milky bar."

I bend to smile and look in Maudy's eyes, and
I tell her "Don't you ever try that trick again.
You gave as such a scare, and you are much too weak
to walk alone." She reaches out to touch my cheek
with a filthy hand!

I must not flinch away, I kiss her brow instead,
but cannot wait to scrub my face, out at the sink.
Then Pat comes out and puts her arm around me. There
are tears in her eyes, and Tilly says, "I think
I wet the bed."

Repartee

Oh great! What fun! An argument in verse!
I can't resist a challenge, count me in!
But let's be civilised, there's nothing worse
than blood 'n' guts out on the floor; let's grin
and bear our disappointments, and reflect
upon the fact this forum's meant to serve
to perpetrate the sonnet, with respect
to both the form and persons: both deserve
the best that we can give. Now, Mr Hall
I'd like to bid you welcome. We are quite
impassioned as you see, but after all
this is the place to find the erudite
in sonneteers. Ask anyone. It's true.
We usually are friendly too. Are you?

Risham Piriri

Accommodation's sparse along the track
To Kathmandu. I ache, I'm caked with dirt,
I'm sick of 'up' and long to hit the sack.
It's getting dark. The Himalayas flirt
with us; we catch a glimpse of sunlit snow
behind the mist that rises every dusk.
The hut is smoothed with mud; it's no chateau,
its ambience a charming goaty musk.
But 'risham piriri' the local sing,
For life's a scarf that's borne upon the wind,
a sometimes laughing sometimes crying thing;
surrender; God will not be disciplined.
I couldn't give a yak-pat what they think,
Provided I can sleep despite the stink.

Sand Crab and Muddy (super-long sonnet)

Two crabs were friends, one from the better part
of sea, i.e. the sand, who lived the high
life high on life decaying a la carte.
The other crab, who came from mud, would try
to emulate his mate, though he was drab,
and rather staid. Now when they died, the two
were parted; one to Heaven, one to crab
about in Hell. The anguished Muddy threw

himself upon the mercy of a saint
who gave permission for a sideways trip
on down. He scuttled off with no restraint
except the stern directive not to slip
and slide too long. "Be back by ten and bring
your harp. Don't carp to me if you should fail;
your tail will fry and so will I; that thing
is all you've got to swing the Gate." So, pale,

his palps a-tating, Muddy went and found
his sand crab buddy all het up in hell.
He had a disco there! He'd been around
as well; mudcrab boozed right outta his shell,
he danced, he sang and played. But then, dismayed,
he saw the time had gone. "Goodbye dear sand,
I must away (hick) I'm afraid I've stayed
too long." At Heaven's Gate, a reprimand:

the Saint Bernard said "No, you can't come in.
Now listen mate, I told you don't be late,
and where's your harp?" "Oh please, I'm fulla gin,
have mercy pal, I can't recall... oh wait

I think I do remember this though;
I left my harp in Sand Crab's disco."

Scarecrow Fair – sonnet for Barry, Matt and Travis

Now young folk gather for this festival.
They are a scruffy lot, in knitted hats
and sandals, ragged coats against the chill,
both sexes wearing feathers. Some have mats
as if they've come to pray. Inside they've set
up stalls; recycled clothes and books, some art,
a place behind a veil where you can get
an Oriental massage. There's a part
with tables for petitions: save the trees,
the land. Musicians come and go, they sing
of eagles, oceans, mountains, tigers... pleas
to stop the carnage, start reforesting.
At last I understand, at last admire
this people's army in defence of Gaia.

Seasons of the Moon

Through all the long strong seasons of the moon
I've wandered wistful, yearning for his touch.
In all the empty spaces placed in front of me
where he can never be, I mourn.

For all the poems he will never share,
for secrets, songs and sounds he'll never know,
and for the moon that shone in glory when he died
I've cried the many months since he was gone.

Through all the bright bold silvered nights
the moon has dressed in loveliness he'll never see,
and all our lost tomorrows wrapped in sorrow
I will still love him tenderly.

Sensual

Beside the road a foxhound sits to wait,
his back a leaning warmth towards his Man.
The sunlight catches fur, immaculate
and fine; a sheen of white, of black and tan.
His silky head rests gently on the arm
he trusts, his ears are soft with fuzzy down,
his neck a line of simple graceful charm
where seams of fur describe a richer brown.
I long to fondle him but fear his teeth,
for wolfish instincts even of a pet
still crouch in savage passion there beneath
this sweet facade. I mustn't stop. And yet
although I do not dare disturb his calm,
the ghost of feeling paints upon my palm.

Singapore Cats

A rattan basket full of kittens, every one deformed –
a crooked tail, an ear turned to the head.
It is the way in Singapore, for I have heard it said
that if a perfect cat should leap a body
it becomes undead.

Pontianak! Pontianak!
hair at the front!
face at the back!
gobbles children!
eats anak!
anak-a-snack!
Pontianak, Pontianak!
crack-crack!

In Singapore you never see a perfect pussy cat
a cat must always have a nasty flaw,
if not a crumpled ear or tail they may rip out a claw
or maybe very many; put an eye out
also, to be sure.

Pontianak! Pontianak!
hair at the front!
face at the back!
Can you listen?
Can you hear?
Get the cat with the crumpled ear!

NB – anak means 'child' in Indonesian.

Singapore Dog

Filthy crippled sweet-faced bitch
ragged threadbare fur,
flesh eroding over bones,
dying by degrees;
panting by the taxis
at Nee Soon.

Shadows gather at her paws
shadeless as the trees;
mercilessness
will dry her dead
as surely as the dictates
of social laws.

In a chipped enamel dish
I bring her water, bring her food,
though every day they steal the plate
I every day restore.

But she at last begins to frisk
and it is not too late.
Now the barking word for dog follows me.

"Gow-lady, here she come…"
"Your gow a lucky one."
It seems the hand of fate that moves my own
has changed her karma now,
and everybody feeds my gow.

She recovers day by day, and then
I hear a merchant say,
"Ha ha! She make baby; gow-kien,"

and graphically he shows me how,
as if I wouldn't know 'til now.

Four puppies scramble in the dust
underneath the taxi-box,
audaciously she bore them all,
against the odds
when given slim advantage
defying human gods
to win their trust.

Four puppies crushed beneath the wheels
not even worthy of a care.
I could have spared them agony
had I not been there
imposing values from another world
judging from my culture's point of view.

She would have died,
quiet in the dust.

I only forced her
fate anew.

Social Honesty and Other Dangers

I am afraid that I will throw myself beneath the train.
The fear of it draws me wickedly;
in projected memory I feel the impact,
(insect on a grid,)
my bones are matches snapped, my flesh is crushed,
(a penny on the line).

Why does danger pull us to the edge of meaning,
though life is precious and our feet are safe on solid ground?
Why does the cliff edge beckon, the deeps malign
call out, the hot-plate dare my palm to sear?

I am afraid that I will jump beneath the train.

Speaking Chinese

How strange to hear my little children speak Chinese,
just piping out amazing sounds like chiming birds.
How little I may know, my adult brain is slow;
I only catch a smattering of oft-said words.

But slowly I begin to notice that they tease
our amah, Kim. They mock her halting English, and
they anglicise Hokkien. I resolve to watch them then.
They take advantage when she doesn't understand.

We take some blankets to the hill, at end of day.
We find a place to watch the stars and talk of space,
and finding far-off worlds that differ from our own
where people wait to greet us in a distant place.

But you will never be the ones we choose, I say,
you'll never go to speak to people living there
because of late I see you have no sympathy.
You can't begin to understand unless you care.

Su-Su

Tip-toed,
arched and bristled
flat-eared and wedge-faced
sabre-toothed
Su-su screams
blazing hate!

"Intruder, submit or die!
How dare you venture
on my turf!
I'll have your throat!"

Glaring ice blue malice,
ululating howls
rippling growls
strutting stiff-legged
evil unleashed!
Su-su the cat!

"Give in
or my mother
will kill you!

Here she comes,

goodbye!"

The Dragon and the Maiden

The dragon breathes and in caressing air
a maiden stirs with dreams of succubi.
A butterfly alights upon her hair
beneath the dragon's rainbow-spangled eye.
The time has come for alchemy to wake
an ancient magic beautiful and wild,
arranging chemicals within to make
incredibly, a woman from a child.
Transforming as was ever meant to be,
the dragon is her body, which is wise,
that she has always loved and always will,
and now she sees it glittering arise.
Enchanted at the brink of adulthood
she scintillates with beauty, as she should.

The Eel

On a shoulder shrugging sea
alone
I fished a high and narrow stream
dividing stone
and cried for forces that had cleft
a dream I couldn't hold;

childhood shackled,
dragging chains
of tangled adolescent mystery.
Everything had changed.

From the water at my knee
I pulled an eel,
black as shadow, silvered green,
his shining body strong. He fought with me,

he struggled wildly on the stone
and turned back constantly
determined to be free.

I stripped my blouse
and tied it, hoisted him within.
He pushed and writhed against my thigh
all the while I hefted him,
across the miles
to home.

Far
from his deep and hidden place
he tried all night
to find the image in his head,

he slid across the grass,
he turned his body and his iron face
again, again,

in yearning for the lead-dark depth,
to lie
where he belonged.

I took him back at dawn.
He knew the way
across the stone.

The water shimmered,
sliver-skin
between two worlds,
his own beneath...

He slid
a mirror opened, shivered.

He was gone.

The Tale of Sir Reginald

Reginald rebuffed me at the start
when I asked if I could call him Reg.
"My name is Reginald," said he,
"You will address me properly.
You are just a nurse so play your part!"

Angrily he told me who was boss,
and how he felt about the likes of me.
But he knew and so did I
that he had come to us to die.
Little things like that can make you cross.

Thus he and I began a little game,
shocking and audacious on that day;
It rather took him by surprise
as I gasped and dropped my eyes,
bowed and called him by his proper name.

"Sir Reginald,' I said and curtsied low,
"Sir Reginald' I said, hand to my heart,
"It's altogether plain to see
though you're a man of quality
I am just a nurse so how was I to know?'

Starting with his eyes a smile began
and it was fairly clear we both would win;
I stuck my lip out in a pout
hammed it till his laugh rang out
delighted to become a knighted man.

The game between us rapidly progressed
we took delight in playing each our part.

No one could really miss it!
He'd take my hand and kiss it!
The visitors were very much impressed!

"That fellow by the window is a knight!
 Listen, you will hear them call him Sir."
(For everyone who saw his glee
addressed him just the same as me,)
his eyes would fairly sparkle with delight!

We still recall Sir Reginald with love
for yes, he left us long ago.
Although the body dies
the human spirit flies!
That is why its symbol is a dove.

Till We Part

He leans. I help him, shut the car
and say,

"Let us go now, you and I."

He's so wasted in his chair.
I push him up the hill.

Wheels turn, turn, turn.

He replies
"For I have promises to keep
and miles to go before I sleep…"

We repeat
"and miles to go before I sleep."

It is his last, weary trip to the hospital.

There are no more promises, my love.

Time Flux

What happened to that thing I put away?
It isn't where I know it's always been!
I saw it only just the other day,
around the time I had a little clean…
It's cleaning up that does it every time!
Why can't I leave things well enough alone?
Whenever I declutter, dust and shine,
it zaps 'em clear into the Twilight Zone!
Where time and space pretend to other rules,
where socks and earrings sneak away to hide.
I wonder if there's many other fools
who tidy things into a fluxing tide?
Perhaps it also works the other way;
you'll never guess what I found yesterday!

Tiny Gecko

A sandy-coloured gecko slowly creeps
upon the hospice floor.
What are you doing here? There is no food for you;
your relatives don't come inside.
Flies are an anathema.
The things that they can do
have made me weep.
Kept me from sleep.
Too true.

Perfect little sandy feet are ridged to climb.
A termite's breath their touch within my palm,
but your tiny belly's hollow as reverse parenthesis
concaves almost touching. I won't let you die.
Slight your sliver-body, round your eyes
gazing from the glassy plastic jar.
BIOLOGICAL SPECIMEN it says;
indeed, you are.

Sandy little gecko, you are free at last.
Safe in my mosquito-garden wild
as dreams, all danger past.
Run to the rocks and hide,
run away and live
my little gecko-child.

To Each Their Own

Cicada drumsong thrums hypnotically,
besotted birds beguile with season's songs;
desire evokes desire specifically
designed to stir a mate; to each belongs
a special cry. Sound ribbons thread the air
when cats are on the make, koalas roar,
frogs' water-voices break in bright despair.
Each creature to its own's a troubadour.
When beings bawl for partners and for space,
and mothers call to keep in touch with young,
the world resounds with din in every place
since coupled reproduction was begun.
The urge may be the sweetest agony,
yet but for sex how silent life would be.

What Kind of Light?

What kind of light am I?
I'm not a beacon, (though I'd like to be),
I'm not a light-house guiding ships across the sea
I'm not an arc-light, splitting wide the sky.
What kind of light am I?

What would I like to be?
No, not a lime-light; I don't like a scene,
no, not a welding light, (oxyacetylene),
and not a strobe light, flashing's not for me.
What would I like to be?

What kind of light? Let's see…
I'm not a chandelier, swinging high,
A flare? Too bright. A heater? Far too hot and dry.
An X-ray? No. I value privacy.
What kind of light? Let's see…

What kind of light? I know,
I'm just a little lamp like Florence had
to comfort and to soothe folks, when they're feeling bad,
and show the way for faithful feet to go.
What kind of light? I know.

Wufflegrot Series

Introducing The Wufflegrot

There is a beast with azure fur,
it is the Wufflegrot of Mer,
which hides with much proficiency
within a blue as blue can be.

The Wufflegrot is quite a pest,
it has the power of arrest.
It likes to ambush folk like me,
and take away their poetry.

Now it can pounce at any time,
attracted by the sound of rhyme,
then no one else but you can see
you're just as blue as blue can be.

Though it can boing from any place
its sense of timing's a disgrace;
it makes your meter history,
a missed and misty mystery.

The thing that it most likes to do,
is take your muse away from you;
'cos it will hit you with its gun
and eat your poems on the run.

Then every other shade that was
begins to fade away because
they're sinking in a dismal sea
that's just as blue as blue can be.

So when the Wufflegrots abound
you gotta look for them around.
So buy my Wufflegrotarie,
go get'em with impunity!

Grots in the Grot

It's got a snuffly kind of wuffle which it wiffles night and day
like sniffing for a truffle,
so they say.
It will snork a gawky porker or a morky night-time walker,
with a shimmy and a shuffle
it will steal your rhymes away.

Alert!

I saw a Wufflegrot today, hiding in the sky.
I would have wandered near it but it sneezed.
It sneezed and squeezed a bluish drop of malice from its eye.
I'm very glad I saw it,
I was pleased.

It dappled down into a tree above the passers by,
and hefted something purple like a dart,
a stripey stringy whirl around a curly kind of fly
that didn't look offensive;
it was smart.

I know a bit about the beast and how it makes you shy;
the Wufflegrot has robbed me many times
for it has pounced and bounced me and in trouncing made me cry;
the Wufflegrot has always
got my rhymes.

With fur of such a pretty shade of lapis lazuli
it loves to crunch a lunch of poetry
what it will do is make you blue then it will satisfy
its hunger so I think that I
will flee.

It's really rather saddish when you come to reason why
a wufflething would snuffle up our dreams
I thought I saw a bruisy blitty splish of bluish dye
and oh oh

yes I
thought it would follow me.
Damn.

Wuffle-isations

HELP!

It was rubbing its tummy and looking at me.
I thought what a bother! And ran.
My poems are yummy, that's plain as can be,
he's the Wuffle that wants 'em. Oh damn.

Wufflegrot Dispelling By Mis-spelling

You may comment that my spelling is atrocious,
you may chuckle at the silly gaffs I make,
but you've noticed that I'm lately so loquacious;
let me say that nothing happened by mistake.

I have met a mythic monster that'll break your heart.
Here's a fact I've often noticed to be true;
when you're producing stuff that's obviously smart
herds of hungry Wufflegrots will go for you.

Whereas writing perfect poems may be seductive,
they'll surely bring the beast which eats afflatus
therefore should you really want to stay productive
add the odd errata literatus!

Kathy's Coet – by Jude

Kathy had a little Coet,
sweetly tied with yellow string,
seeing that she was a poet
it began to sweetly sing:
"O humankinds are lovesome whos,
who chooses yellows, not those blues!"

And so the Coet, funny thing,
continued on to coo and sing.
Sunshine flowing from its fingers
made the air around it gleam.
Kathy thought… "I hope it lingers,"
giving it a Kathy beam.

But Coet, sadly waved bye bye,
it said, "I bluely have to fly."
Then Kathy saw where it had got
right snaffled by the Wufflegrot!
Wuffle's got a little Coet
tightly tied with dark blue string.

Wuffle said, "Beware of poets,
they're as mad as anything!
O humankinds are droobful whos,
who chooses yellows over blues!"
Is what the Wuffle told the Coet,
to stop it singing to its poet.

Somewhere in a dim blue closet
tangled in a bluish cloud
there's a creature heard to posit
singing in a voice not loud:

"O humankinds are droobful whos
an' this is why I sings the blues,
I tried to beat the Wufflegrot,
but this closet's where I got."

Searching For My Coet

Cooee! Cooee! Oh Coet answer me
for I am lost and limp without your songs,
if I can only find your string
oh I will pull like anything
to get you back in my bivouac
where you belongs.

Bereft! Bereft! My little heart is cleft;
intent I run from closet door to door,
I'm sick with such a sadling thing,
but what is that a-glistening?
A dinky dob, a bluish blob
of Wuffle spoor!

Hurray! Hurray! Now I am on my way!
The Wuffle's left a trail for me to find.
(So this is why it's called a grot;
the Wuffle leaves its poohs a lot)
and such pretty shiny poozes
that are made of lovely muses
all crystallined.

Kazoong! Kazzing! My heart begins to sing,
a curly piece of string is on the floor,
and with a sense of destiny
I hear the Coet answer me;
"Yes I am here but oh I fear
you will not want to have me near
you anymore.

Oh woe is me! I dread for you to see!
I'm not the Coet that I was before,

I have been changed, I'm rearranged,
addicted to the Wuffle spoor!
Now I'll pester every poet,
and they'll know the name of Coet
for evermore.

Oh don't come near! Oh poet you must fear
the Coet lest my lust take awful flight
for I will make you write and write
I will disturb your sleep at night
composing for that Wuffle thing
to snaffle with its curly string.
It isn't right."

HAIKU

head lice
a bird picks spiders
from the eaves

white blossoms
star
the dark wet earth

new year's
storm chorus—
an alarm of dogs

darkness
a frog calls
I am

shadows
chase their birds
into sunset

on the TV aerial
a myna bird
broadcasts

spring's herald
shines with sunshine
on his scales

autumn rain—
ducks plow ripples
under circles

pink earth
white snow
a pigeon's breast

pinecone embers–
dreams of forests turned
to ash

shadow butterflies
by shadow trees–
petals fall

distant thunder–
two tree frogs emerge
from the letter box

mist
one by one
each boat alone

sunrise
a golden orb weaver
catches fire

again so tenderly
the mother falcon's
beak

after the storm
new nests from old—
so many robbers

poor hermit crab—
without another's shell
you die

honey bees—
headfirst into
sweetness

summer breeze—
caterpillar Tarzans swing
to the next tree

caught
in the tree next door
the moon

pink and golden
palm nut blossoms droop
with bees

prayer wheel—
a dry leaf spins
on a cobweb

empty nest
her bones beneath the tree—
dew-fall

rain at last
a gecko licks its eye

daisy seeds fly
above
the mower

oh koala
you were a termite's nest
until you moved

on every leaf
a shining ball—
nasturtiums in the rain

new red leaves—
the lilly pilly yearns
for spring

little flowers;
a stick-still insect
spears a bee

dry roots
trees are dirty dancing
in the wind

a rainbow
after the flood–
kookaburras laugh

last light–
one tree top
gilded

high cliff–
a new shoot
trembles

vacuum cleaning–
an echidna's
tongue

sunlight rolls
through the lens of a wave
to the sea floor

beachcombing–
jellyfish made of ocean
stranded next to it

SENYRU

dad and I
heart high in the trout-stream
for the last time

                              dappled moonlight—
                              memories come
                              and go

a shadow
walks in shadow—
my friend

                              the backpack—
                              taking turns to carry
                              his ashes

lost sons—
smoke drifts and is gone
in winter wind

                              gathering thoughts—
                              a column of tiny insects
                              weave in dance

nicotine cravings—
deadly nightshade grows
through concrete

                    midnight swim–
                    we float between
                    infinities

a fish
takes the mosquito
that took my blood

                    fisherman—
                    up before the flies
                    cleaning his catch

dandelion clock–
an old woman's
careful hairdo

                    gentle waves–
                    can we forgive you
                    for yesterday?

that little boy
at the water's edge–
his face in the sand

                    cancer–
                    panic haunts the space
                    between us

cold snap—
under the quilt with me
his ashes

zen—
a swirl of water
there go I

circling
the starving child—
photographers

epiphany—
a bird lands
in its shadow

we found a skull
and watched in the rain
as the poor thing cried

stonehenge—
wind ripples
the old man's hair

blossoms bob
above the swing
of her ponytail

head lice
a bird picks spiders
from the eaves

                              more rainbows
                    dazzling as they land to feed
                          in a bottlebrush tree

scarecrow
dressed as me
alone

                                  one by one
                             we pass his ashes
                                   to the sea

COVID-19 SENYRU

filthy lucre
from hand to hand
with viruses

together apart
in cyberspace—
haiku

gidday—
smiles flow between
our distances

viruses—
little things
mean a lot

under threat
that leaf in rushing water
on a rock

sign language—
feigned self-defensiveness
and blown kisses

air handshakes
heel and elbow bumps
as we pass

panic over—
supermarket shelves
full again

somehow
we see the smiles
behind masks

In memory of my husband,
Peter William Earsman

Anzac Day

It's Anzac Day tomorrow. In Australia and New Zealand, people will meet at dawn to remember our fallen warriors. There will be parades of veterans down closed streets, the air will be full of tension and military music and there will be palpable comradery between soldiers, as there has ever been.

People line the streets to cheer and wave flags. There's continuous coverage on TV.

I jostle through the crowds that thicken at the edge of the road, run to keep up, hungry for the sight of you; once-red hair shines white in the sun; you stride in time, your back straight, your head held high; swept away as you were 30 years ago, bound for Vietnam.

Larry and Don carry a Kiwi banner, drawn by our son from the tattoo on your arm.

My first migraine begins, fractured faces move in splintered glass.

We meet later with other veterans, to sing, to drink and tell stories. Never of Vietnam though, never of scars. We laugh a lot, understanding things unspoken, knowing that the poison runs inside us all.

Tommy Tuhoro slaps his thighs. "Hit 'em really hard," he says, "Really hard." Slap, slap, "Kamate kamate Hora! Hora!" He teaches us the Maori war dance famous at football matches. I smack hard, proud to be here; the Haka burns my skin, lifts my heart with pride and warms it with love.

Guitars draw us together, we sing Waiata and sixties songs, blending our voices in familiar melodies and dancing if we can, in the old ways.

It will be Anzac Day tomorrow.

I remember your coffin, strewn with red poppies. The boys and I stand at your head
nodding and smiling at your friends who bring a tribute blossom, one by one.

One by one they fall as men will fall like Agent Orange droplets on your
skin, inhaled, ingested, taken in from friendly hands to kill by stealth in
tumours now the world's forgotten Vietnam.
Goddamn! They took the risk as soldiers do, but poison is another thing.

it's nearly Anzac Day –
at dawn when people meet
will you throw a poppy
in the bay for him?

ACKNOWLEDGEMENTS

Over the years, my husband Peter and I made many friends in the poetry community around the world. Although there are too many people to thank here, I would like to mention some who supported us in our poetry.

They include: Pris Campbell, Dennis Gobou, Michael Dylan Welch, Lynne Rees, Beverley George, Michael Rehling, Peter Moltoni, Moira Richards, Sprite London, Mary White, Linda Papanicolaou, Denis Homes, Carol Raisfeld, Laryalee Fraser, Judie Peet, Denise Curran, Carol Raisfeld, Geoff Sanderson, Myron Lysenko, Mike Keville, Carole MacRury, Ron C. Moss, Norman Darlington, Freda Edis, David Gwylem Anthony, Mike Alexander, Dave McClure, Alan Wickes, Ann Drysdale, Eric Bloomquest, Jan Iwaszkiewicz, Margaret Griffiths, Werner and Jane Reichold, John William Knight, Hidenori Hiruta, John Carley, Toru Tanaka, Michael Dillon-Welch, Eiko Yachimoto, Amanda Stansell Rushing, Mary Kendall, Janice Bostock, Lynne Sanders-Braithwaite, Berenice Lydia Dunford.

There are many more whom I have doubtlessly missed, and if that is the case then please know that I appreciate you. I am fortunate to have had so much love and friendship in my life and am grateful for the support of my family and friends.